Jim Arnosky's

L ABOUT Manatees

SCHOLASTIC NONFICTION
an imprint of
SCHOLASTIC

For Jordan and Elliott

ISBN-13: 978-0-439-90361-5
ISBN-10: 0-439-90361-0

Printed in the USA   23

First Scholastic paperback printing, May 2008
The text type was set in 16 point Raleigh.

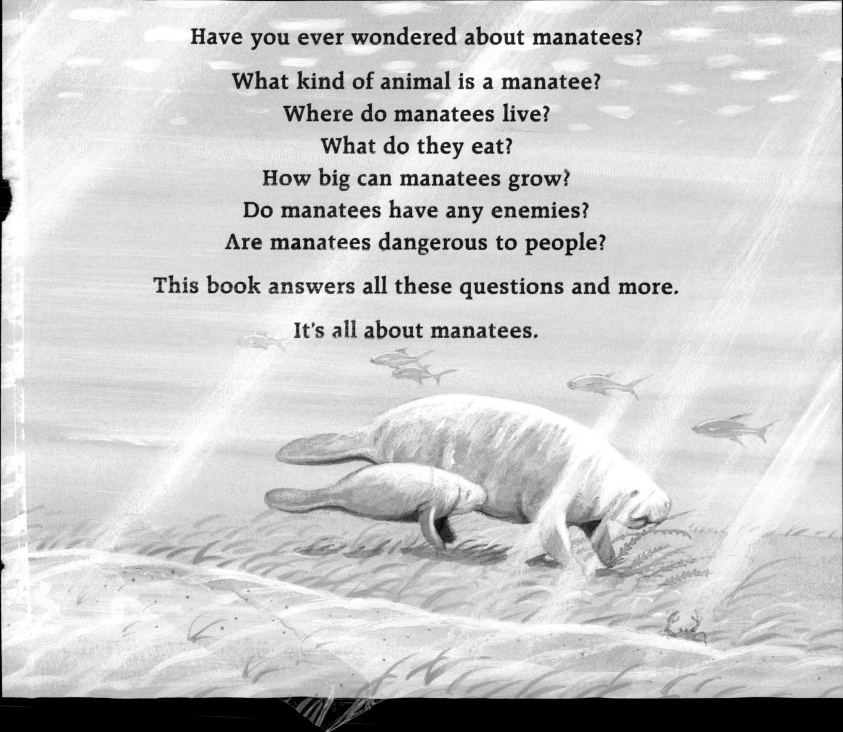

Have you ever wondered about manatees?

What kind of animal is a manatee?
Where do manatees live?
What do they eat?
How big can manatees grow?
Do manatees have any enemies?
Are manatees dangerous to people?

This book answers all these questions and more.

It's all about manatees.

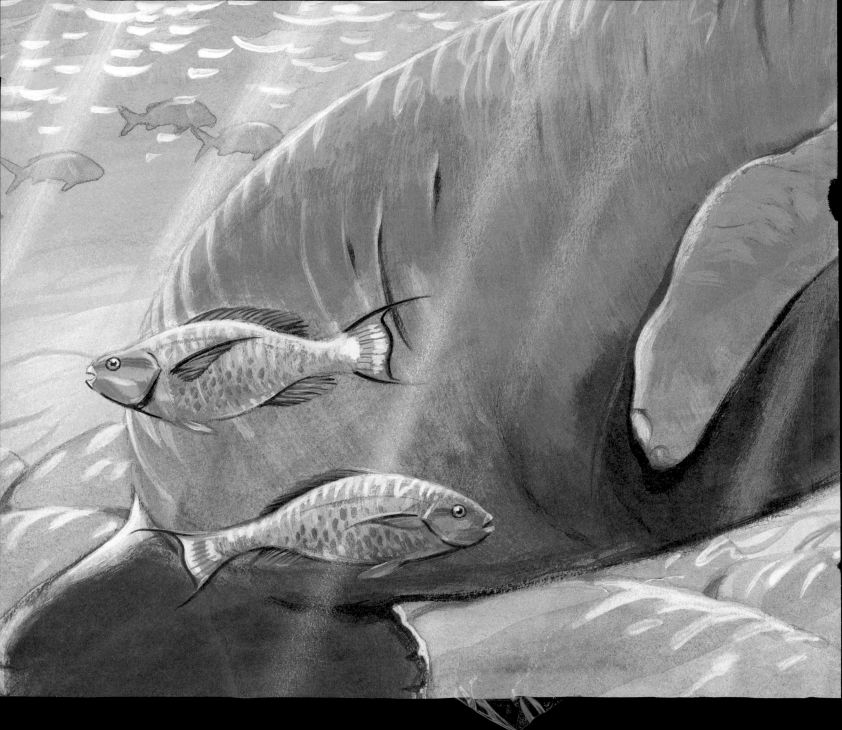

Manatees are large
mammals that live in warm
water. They are distantly
related to elephants. You
can see the resemblance in
a manatee's thick gray skin,
fine hairs, and huge body size.
An average fully grown manatee is 10 to 11
feet long and weighs more than 1,000 pounds.
Some individuals grow to be 13 feet long and
weigh more than 3,000 pounds. In captivity, a
manatee can live for decades. We don't know yet
how long wild manatees live.

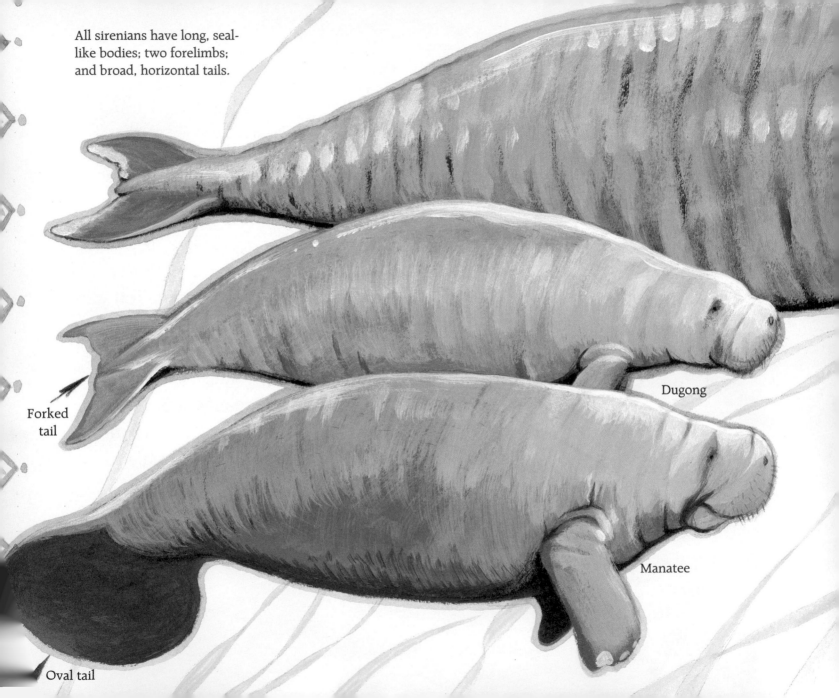

All sirenians have long, seal-like bodies; two forelimbs; and broad, horizontal tails.

Forked tail

Oval tail

Dugong

Manatee

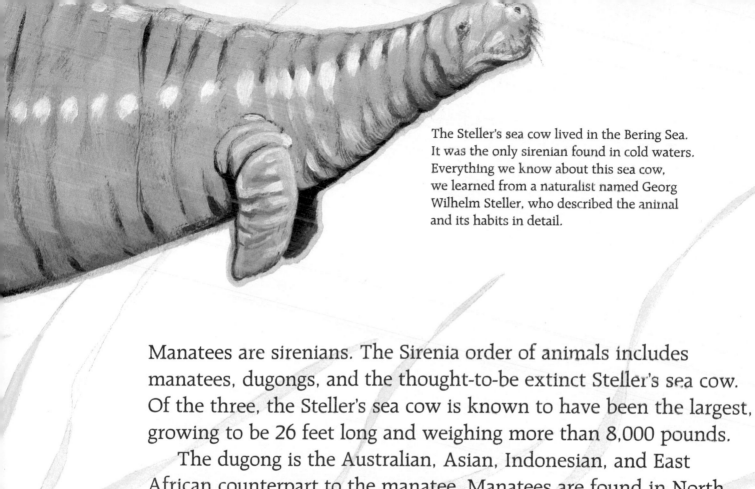

The Steller's sea cow lived in the Bering Sea. It was the only sirenian found in cold waters. Everything we know about this sea cow, we learned from a naturalist named Georg Wilhelm Steller, who described the animal and its habits in detail.

Manatees are sirenians. The Sirenia order of animals includes manatees, dugongs, and the thought-to-be extinct Steller's sea cow. Of the three, the Steller's sea cow is known to have been the largest, growing to be 26 feet long and weighing more than 8,000 pounds.

The dugong is the Australian, Asian, Indonesian, and East African counterpart to the manatee. Manatees are found in North America, the Caribbean Islands, Central America, South America, and West Africa.

The manatees found in the United States are actually West Indian manatees, but they are known as Florida manatees because most of them live year-round in the waters of Florida.

Only about 2,000 of them remain in the wild. Florida manatees live mostly peaceful lives, coexisting with other freshwater and saltwater wildlife.

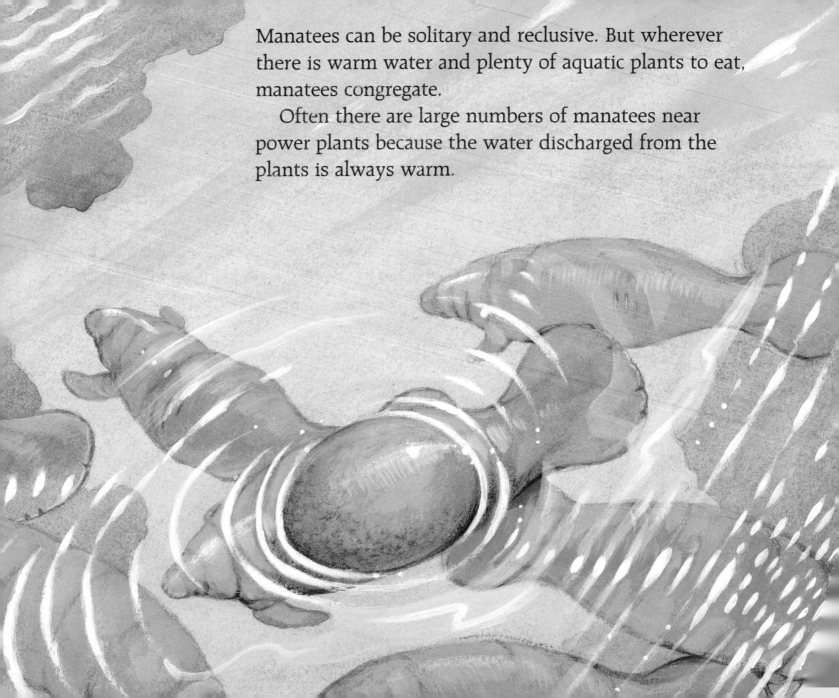

Manatees can be solitary and reclusive. But wherever there is warm water and plenty of aquatic plants to eat, manatees congregate.

Often there are large numbers of manatees near power plants because the water discharged from the plants is always warm.

Like all mammals, manatees breathe air. To breathe, all a manatee needs to do is poke its nostrils out of the water. I locate manatees by scanning the water surface for the sight of a manatee nose popping up.

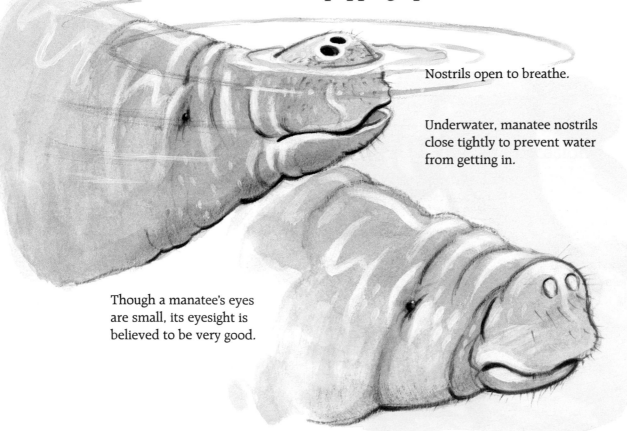

Nostrils open to breathe.

Underwater, manatee nostrils close tightly to prevent water from getting in.

Though a manatee's eyes are small, its eyesight is believed to be very good.

Manatee ears do not show but they can hear sounds underwater and above the surface.

Underwater, a distant manatee appears to be a large blue-gray blob. As it swims nearer, its features slowly become defined. Although their size can be impressive, manatees are gentle and harmless to human swimmers.

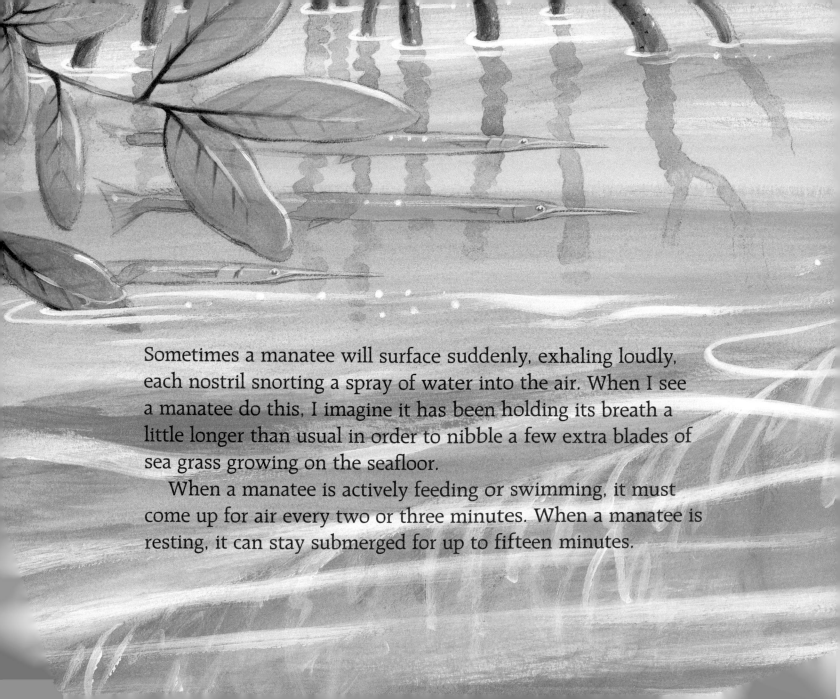

Sometimes a manatee will surface suddenly, exhaling loudly, each nostril snorting a spray of water into the air. When I see a manatee do this, I imagine it has been holding its breath a little longer than usual in order to nibble a few extra blades of sea grass growing on the seafloor.

When a manatee is actively feeding or swimming, it must come up for air every two or three minutes. When a manatee is resting, it can stay submerged for up to fifteen minutes.

A manatee's limbs are not flippers. They are more like arms. Manatees do not have hind limbs, just a broad tail.

The bones in a manatee's limbs are very strong, making the limbs powerful enough to paddle the huge body along.

Manatee limb showing three "fingernails"

Manatees use their limbs to slowly paddle themselves forward or backward. They also use their limbs to pull things such as floating plants close to them.

A manatee uses its highly flexible snout and upper lip to grasp vegetation to eat. Its diet consists entirely of green aquatic plants. Manatees grind up their food with large, flat back teeth called molars. They have no front teeth.

Manatees breed every two to five years and give birth in the water to a single calf. A newborn manatee knows instinctively how to swim and nurse milk at its mother's armpit. Manatees communicate with one another using high-pitched squeaking sounds. A mother manatee makes much softer sounds for her calf to hear. These communications sound almost like murmuring or quiet talking.

Manatee calf
nursing

Manatee calves stay close to
their mothers. As they grow
larger, young manatees venture
away a little on their own,
discovering the watery world
they live in. Manatees neither
threaten nor are threatened by
any other wildlife.

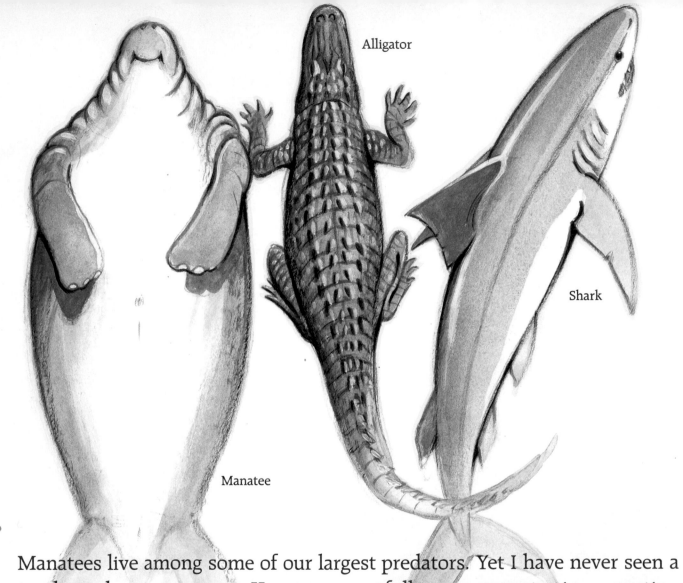

Alligator

Shark

Manatee

Manatees live among some of our largest predators. Yet I have never seen a tooth mark on a manatee. Here you see a full-grown manatee in proportion to a few large predators. The manatee's sheer size and thick skin most likely deter attacks.

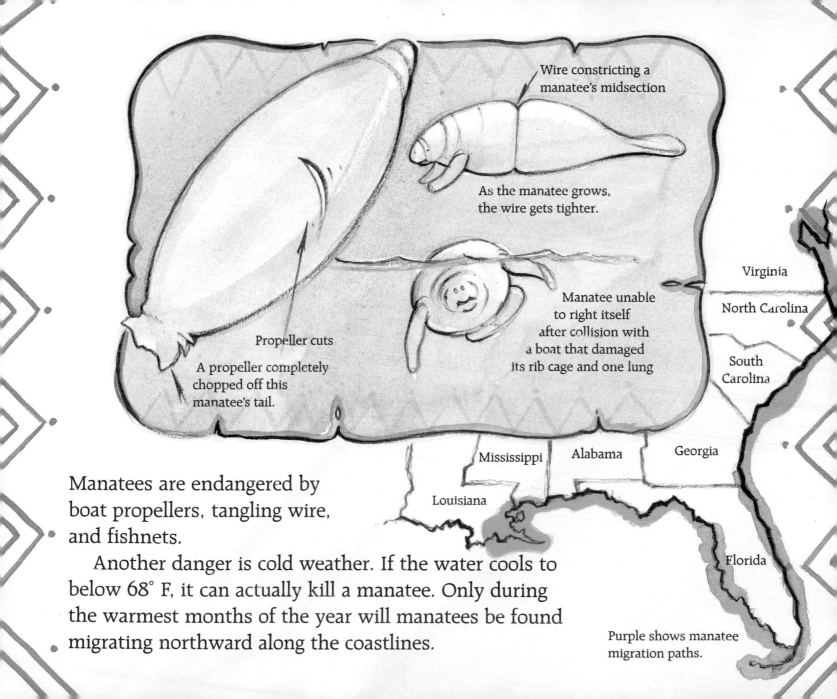

Wire constricting a manatee's midsection

As the manatee grows, the wire gets tighter.

Propeller cuts

A propeller completely chopped off this manatee's tail.

Manatee unable to right itself after collision with a boat that damaged its rib cage and one lung

Virginia

North Carolina

South Carolina

Georgia

Alabama

Mississippi

Louisiana

Florida

Manatees are endangered by boat propellers, tangling wire, and fishnets.

Another danger is cold weather. If the water cools to below 68° F, it can actually kill a manatee. Only during the warmest months of the year will manatees be found migrating northward along the coastlines.

Purple shows manatee migration paths.

Manatees do not actually sleep. They rest suspended in the water or lying on the bottom.

A resting manatee lies motionless, staying underwater for ten- or fifteen-minute intervals, just as long as it does while feeding. Between resting intervals, it will rise to the surface to breathe.

Seeing a manatee in the wild is a special experience. A single manatee can draw a crowd of people who have learned to love and respect manatees.

In Florida, manatee habitats are being marked with warning signs so boaters will know to proceed carefully. Research groups monitor individual manatees to learn more about their movements. And rescue teams are ready to help any manatee reported to be injured or found chilled by cold water.

As long as boaters give manatees plenty of room to swim safely, and as long as the aquatic vegetation manatees depend upon for food is protected, these gentle giants will survive.

Michelle Sherburne

MEET JIM ARNOSKY

Jim Arnosky is the author and illustrator of 98
books about wildlife and nature for children.
He has received numerous honors for his work,
including the American Association for the
Advancement of Science Lifetime Achievement
Award for excellence in science illustration.

For this book, Jim drew on his many years of
careful observation of manatees in their native
habitats. In fact, he and Deanna, his wife and
partner in adventure, have even had a manatee
swim up and leisurely rub its side on their
slowly floating boat.

When they are not traveling to visit schools
and to explore nature, Jim Arnosky and his wife
live in Vermont.